THE LIBRARY OF WHY?

Why Is the Sky Blue?

Marian B. Jacobs, Ph.D

The Rosen Publishing Group's
PowerKids Press™
New York

For my grandsons, Carlos and Gianni.

Published in 1999 by The Rosen Publishing Group, Inc.
29 East 21st Street, New York, NY 10010

First Edition

Book Design: Danielle Primiceri

Photo Credits: Cover © 1996 PhotoDisc, Inc.; pp. 4, 12, 20 © 1994 Image Club Graphics, Inc.; pp. 7, 19, 22 © 1996 PhotoDisc, Inc.; p. 8 © Elizabeth Simoson/FPG International; p. 11 © Seth Dinnerman; pp. 15, 16 © 1997 Digital Vision, Ltd.

Jacobs, Marian B.
    Why is the sky blue? / by Marian B. Jacobs.
       p. cm. — (The library of why?)
    Includes index.
    Summary: Discusses the atmosphere, wavelengths of light, clouds, rainbows, and what causes the sky to be different colors.
    ISBN 0-8239-5271-1
    1. Sky—Juvenile literature. 2. Meteorological optics—Juvenile literature. [1. Sky—Miscellanea. 2. Meteorological optics—Miscellanea. 3. Questions and answers.] I. Title. II. Series.
    QC975.3.J33 1998
    551.56′5—dc21
                                                  97–43894
                                                   CIP

Manufactured in the United States of America
                                                      AC

Contents

What Is the Sky?

When we are outside and look up, we see the sky. The sky is part of our **atmosphere** (AT-mus-feer). The atmosphere is a layer of air that completely surrounds Earth. The air in the atmosphere is made up of different gases, water vapor, and dust **particles** (PAR-tih-kulz).

Not all planets or moons have an atmosphere. For example, our moon does not have an atmosphere. The sky there is always black.

◀ *The atmosphere affects the color of the sky.*

Where Does Light Come from in Nature?

Light is energy that comes from the sun. When sunlight shines on the surface of Earth, the light travels through the atmosphere in waves, just like the waves that move through the ocean. But light waves are so tiny that they are **invisible** (in-VIZ-ih-bul). Light waves moving through the atmosphere make the colors we see in the sky.

Even moonlight comes from the sun. The moon doesn't shine by itself. Sunlight shines on the moon, which acts like a mirror and **reflects** (ree-FLEKTS) the light.

Different light waves make different colors in the sky. ▶

How Are Colors Formed?

Light from the sun is called white light. White light is really a mix of all colors. When we pass sunlight through a triangular block of glass called a **prism** (PRIH-zum), the light is separated into seven colors: red, orange, yellow, green, blue, indigo, and violet.

What makes the different colors? Color is made by different **wavelengths** (WAYV-lenkths) of light. Each color has its own wavelength. Violet and blue have the shortest wavelengths. Red has the longest wavelength.

◄ *The group of colors separated by a prism is called the spectrum.*

What Is Light Scattering?

Light scattering (LYT SKAT-er-ing) is when light gets bounced around by particles in the air. An experiment shows us what light scattering is.

○ First, fill a clear glass with water. You can see straight through that glass of water.

○ Next, stir three or four drops of milk into the water. Now the water looks cloudy. The tiny particles of milk in the water get in the way of the light and scatter it. This is just like the way particles in the atmosphere scatter sunlight.

○ Shine a flashlight against the side of the glass. The light will not shine straight through because milk particles are scattering the light.

The water looks cloudy because the light is scattered. ▶

What Makes the Sky Blue?

The color of the sky is made by sunlight traveling through the atmosphere. Sunlight is scattered by tiny particles in the air. The shorter blue and violet wavelengths are scattered more easily than the longer red and orange wavelengths. This means there are more blue and violet wavelengths in the sky.

So why do we see a blue sky and not a violet sky? Blue wavelengths are easier for our eyes to see than violet wavelengths.

◄ How many different shades of blue can you see in the sky in one day?

How Are the Sky and the Ocean Related?

Some people believe that the sky is blue because it reflects the color of the ocean. This is not true. But did you know that the ocean looks blue because it reflects the color of the sky?

Lake and ocean water look blue for another reason too. When light falls on the surface of the water, the water **absorbs** (ab-ZORBZ) all the wavelengths except blue. The blue wavelengths are reflected so we see the water as blue.

Because blue wavelengths are not absorbed, water naturally looks a little bit blue. ▶

Are There Other Colors in the Sky?

Yes, there are other colors in the sky. Before a thunderstorm the sky may look purple or dark gray. And many people enjoy the beautiful colors in sunsets.

Colors change in the sky as sunlight travels through the atmosphere. Different colors are created when light is scattered by particles and the sun moves to different positions in the sky. Different colors also appear depending on the weather.

◄ *Sunrise and sunset are good times to see many colors mixing in the sky.*

How Can You See White in the Sky?

We know that sunlight is really a mixture of all colors. We also know that the color of the sky is caused by tiny particles scattering more blue and violet wavelengths. But when larger particles scatter light, they scatter the wavelengths of *all* the colors, not just blue.

Clouds are made up of lots of large particles and tiny water droplets. So when light hits a cloud, the water droplets and particles scatter *all* the light and the cloud appears white to us.

Depending on how much dust and water are in a cloud, it can appear white, gray, or almost black. ▶

When Do You See All the Colors in the Sky?

Sometimes you can see all the colors in the sky in a rainbow. Rainbows form right after a rainstorm when sunlight travels through raindrops that are still in the air. The raindrops are large enough to act as prisms and split the sunlight into its different colors.

A rainbow will always form on the side of the sky opposite the sun. Rainbows are curved because raindrops are round. The raindrops bend the sunlight as it goes through them. When light bends, we see its colors in a curved shape.

◀ *The colors in a rainbow will always appear in the same order— from the longest wavelength to the shortest. Red is on top, yellow is in the middle, and violet is at the bottom.*

When Is the Sky Red?

Sometimes the sky turns red or orange at sunset. This is when the sun is low in the sky, at the **horizon** (hor-EYE-zun). Light is moving through the thickest layer of dust particles in the air. Only the longest wavelengths of light rays, the reds and oranges, can move directly through that air.

At sunset, there is little sunlight because the sun is slowly dropping below the horizon. The shorter violet, blue, and green wavelengths are scattered. They mix together and make a gray **twilight** (TWY-lyt).

Glossary

absorb (ab-ZORB) To take up and hold on to something.

atmosphere (AT-mus-feer) The layer of gases that surround Earth.

horizon (hor-EYE-zun) The line where the sky and earth appear to meet.

invisible (in-VIZ-ih-bul) Something you can't see with your eyes.

light scattering (LYT SKAT-er-ing) When light rays strike very small particles, get broken up, tossed about, and sometimes reflected.

particle (PAR-tih-kul) A small piece of something.

prism (PRIH-zum) A triangular block of glass that separates white light into seven colors.

reflect (ree-FLEKT) To throw light back.

twilight (TWY-lyt) Light we see in the sky when the sun is below the horizon, just as night is beginning.

wavelength (WAYV-lenkth) The length of a wave.

Web Sites:

You can learn more about the sky at these Web sites:

http://covis.atmos.uiuc.edu/guide/optics/html/optics1.html

http://comlab.ox.ac.uk/oucl/users/sharon.curtis/pretties.html

23

Index